Dare to Invent

CONTENTS

NATIONAL GEOGRAPHIC School Publishing
Hampton-Brown

Words with **air, are, ear**

Look at each picture. Read the words.

Example:

h**air**

b**ear**

sh**are**

p**ear**

st**air**s

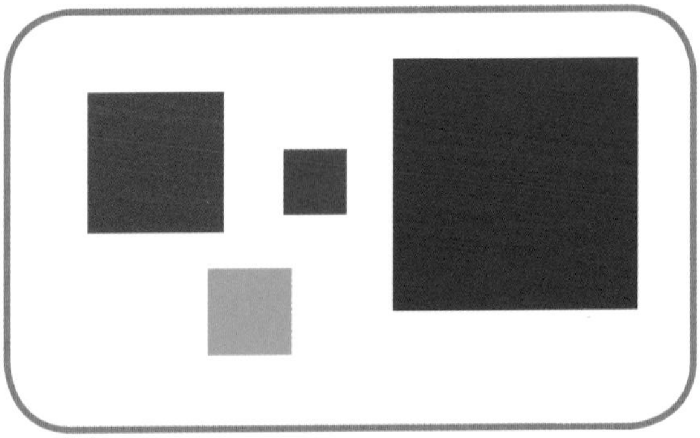

squ**are**s

High Frequency Words

- five
- four
- made
- men
- night
- second
- such
- thought
- well
- wish

Key Words

Read these sentences. Match each sentence to one of the pictures.

Up in the Air

1. **Four men made five** model planes.
2. "I **wish** we could fly them at **night**," said the first man.
3. "Not **such** a smart **thought**," said the **second**.
4. "They don't fly **well** at night," said the third.

What do you think man number four might say?

Phonics Games
NGReach.com

The Little Airplane That Could

by Paula Singh

Orville and Wilbur Wright

In 1903, a pair of men made the first airplane that could fly through the air. They were the Wright brothers. At the end of 1903, one brother got in and flew their airplane 120 feet.

These days, airplanes take off and land in airports. But one hundred years after the Wright brothers' flight, there was another daring flight.

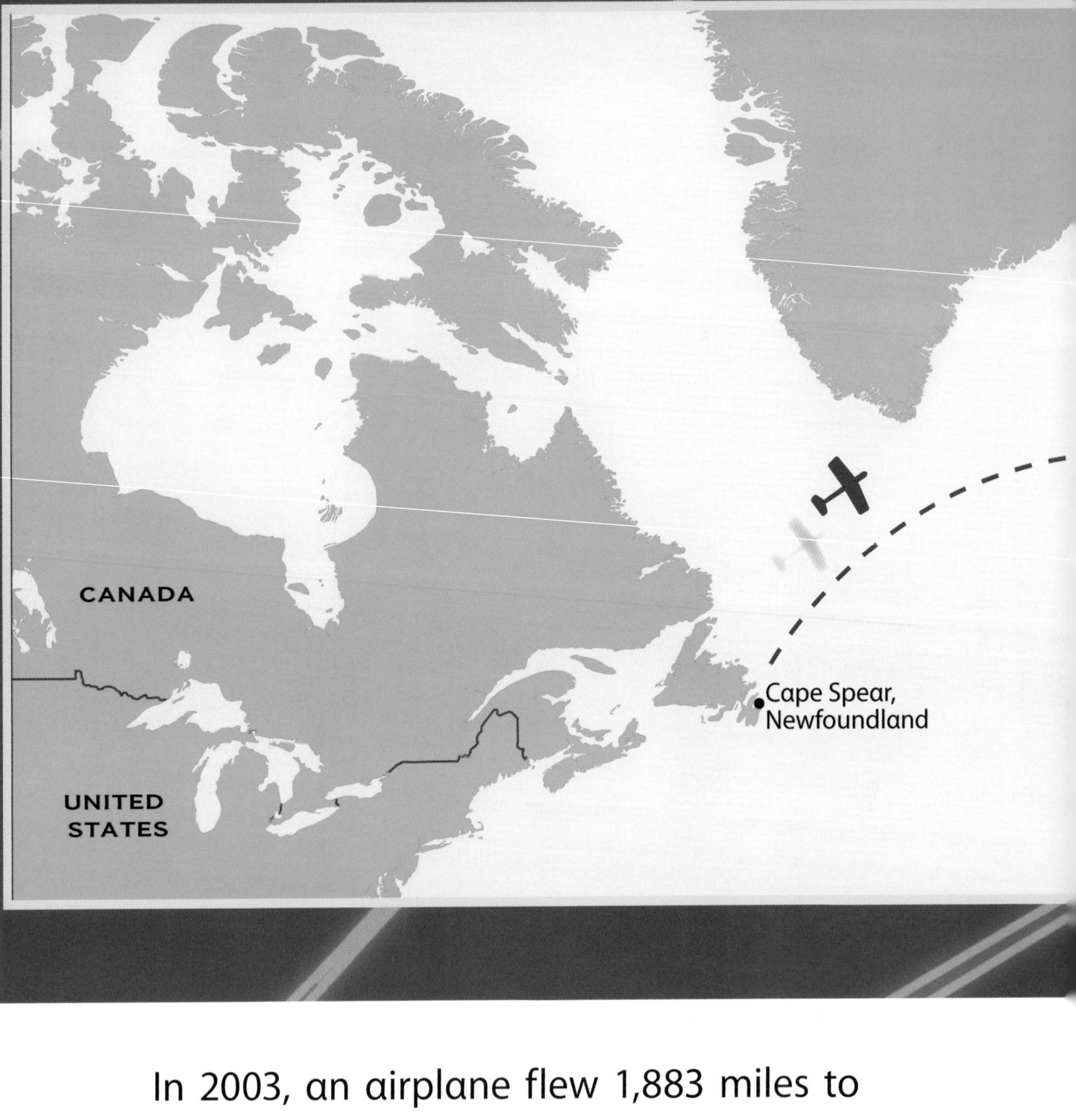

In 2003, an airplane flew 1,883 miles to Ireland. Why was this a rare and daring thing? Why did people care?

This airplane had no pilot. It was six feet long and almost as light as a teddy bear.

It was a model airplane named TAM-5.

Who dared try such a thing?

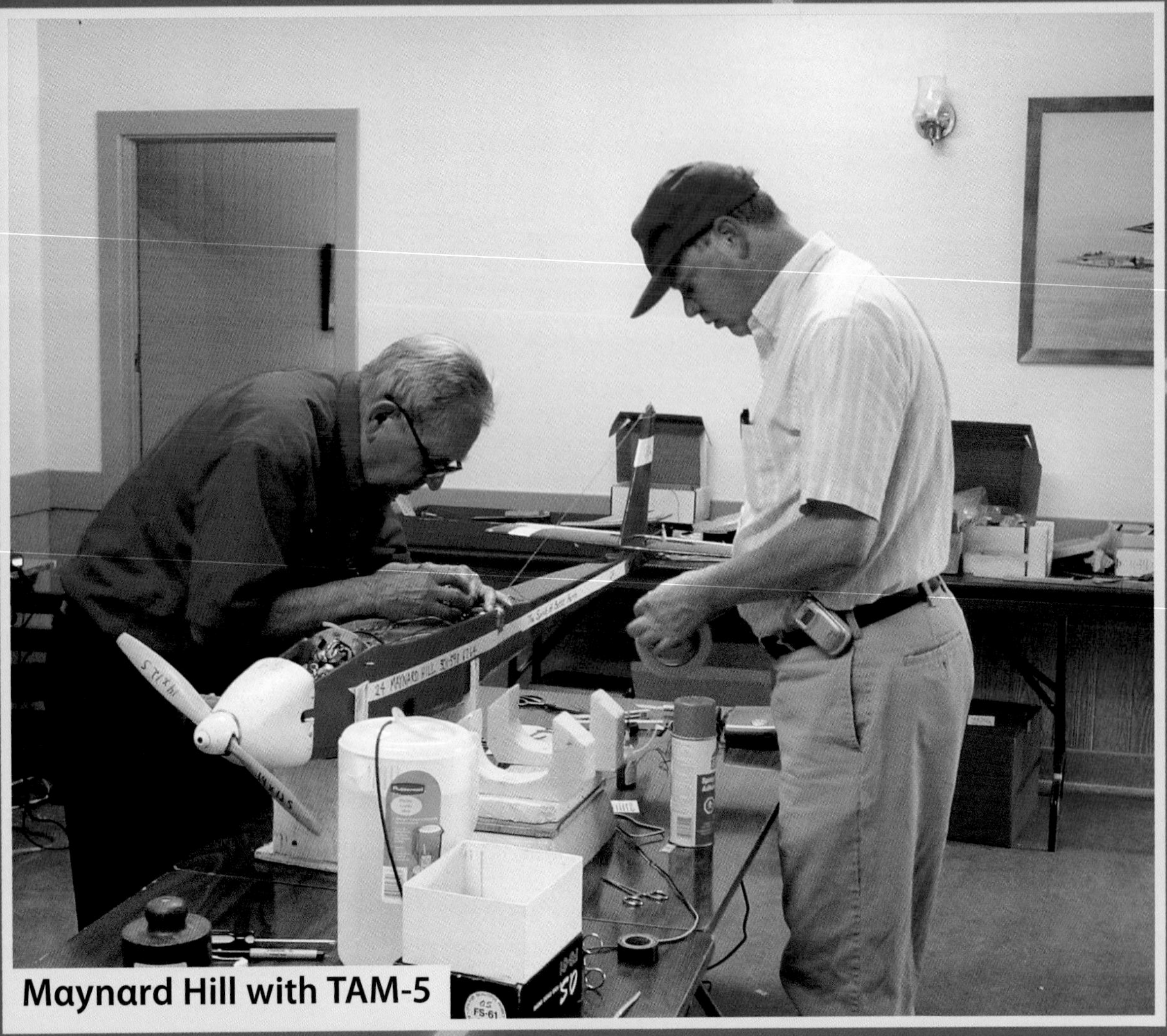
Maynard Hill with TAM-5

Maynard Hill made TAM-5. He'd been making model airplanes most of his life. In 2003, he was 77. He thought he could set the record for longest model-airplane flight.

He needed teams to help him. His plan called for a pair of teams. One was on this side of the ocean. The other was in Ireland.

Hill's airplane needed to be controlled. Team 1 used radio controls to get the plane to 985 feet. Then a "computer pilot" took over. Once it was time to land the airplane in Ireland, the second team took over.

Hill and his teams tried four times to fly model airplanes to Ireland. But their aircraft kept crashing or wearing out around 500 miles.

In late summer in 2003, the teams began flight number five. The airplane took off about 8PM on a cool night. Hill wasn't home in his armchair, letting his teams do all the work. He was with Team 1.

The next two days were a nightmare. Would the little airplane reach Ireland?

The teams had a scare on the second day. They lost contact with the plane.

Team 1 with TAM-5

Team 2 with TAM-5 in Ireland

The team in Ireland stared up at fair skies. At 2PM, TAM-5 came tearing in for a landing!

With his teams' help, Maynard Hill's wish had come true. ❖

Words with **air, are, ear**

Read these words.

bear	chair	circle	air
plane	square	pear	knife

Find words with **air**, **are**, and **ear**.
Use letters to build them.

b e a r

Talk Together

Choose words from the box above to tell your partner what you see in each picture.

The circle is in the square.

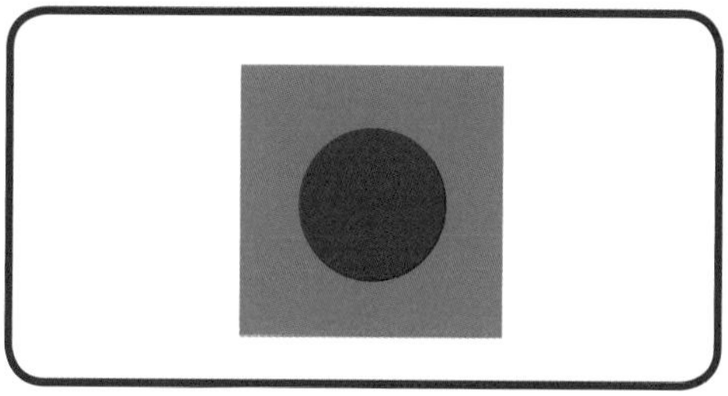

_eer
ear

Words with eer, ear

Look at each picture. Read the words.

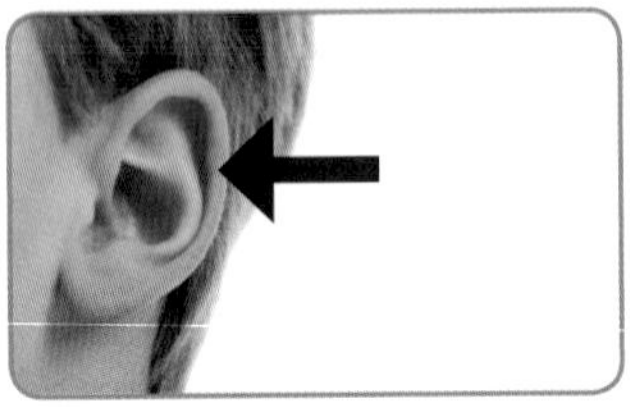

ear

d**eer**

b**ear**d

st**eer**

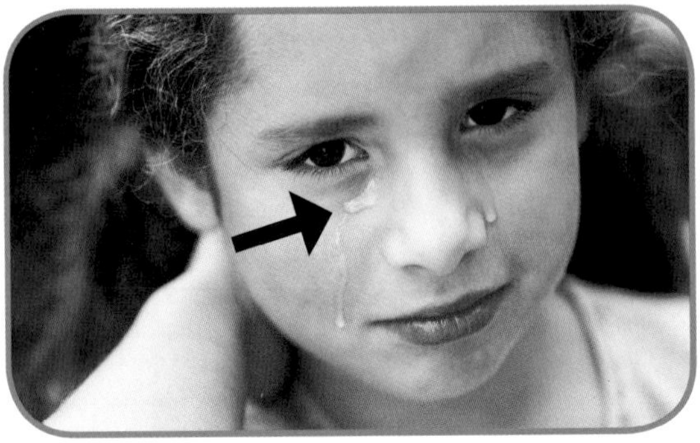

t**ear**s

ch**eer**ing

High Frequency Words
five
four
made
men
night
second
such
thought
well
wish

Key Words

Look at the picture. Read the sentences.

Clare Invents

1. **Five**-year-old Clare **thought** of **four** things to invent.
2. The first helped **men** see **well** at **night**.
3. The **second** **made** a **wish** come true.
4. The other two were not **such** great things!

What did the first thing help the men do at night?

Phonics Games
NGReach.com

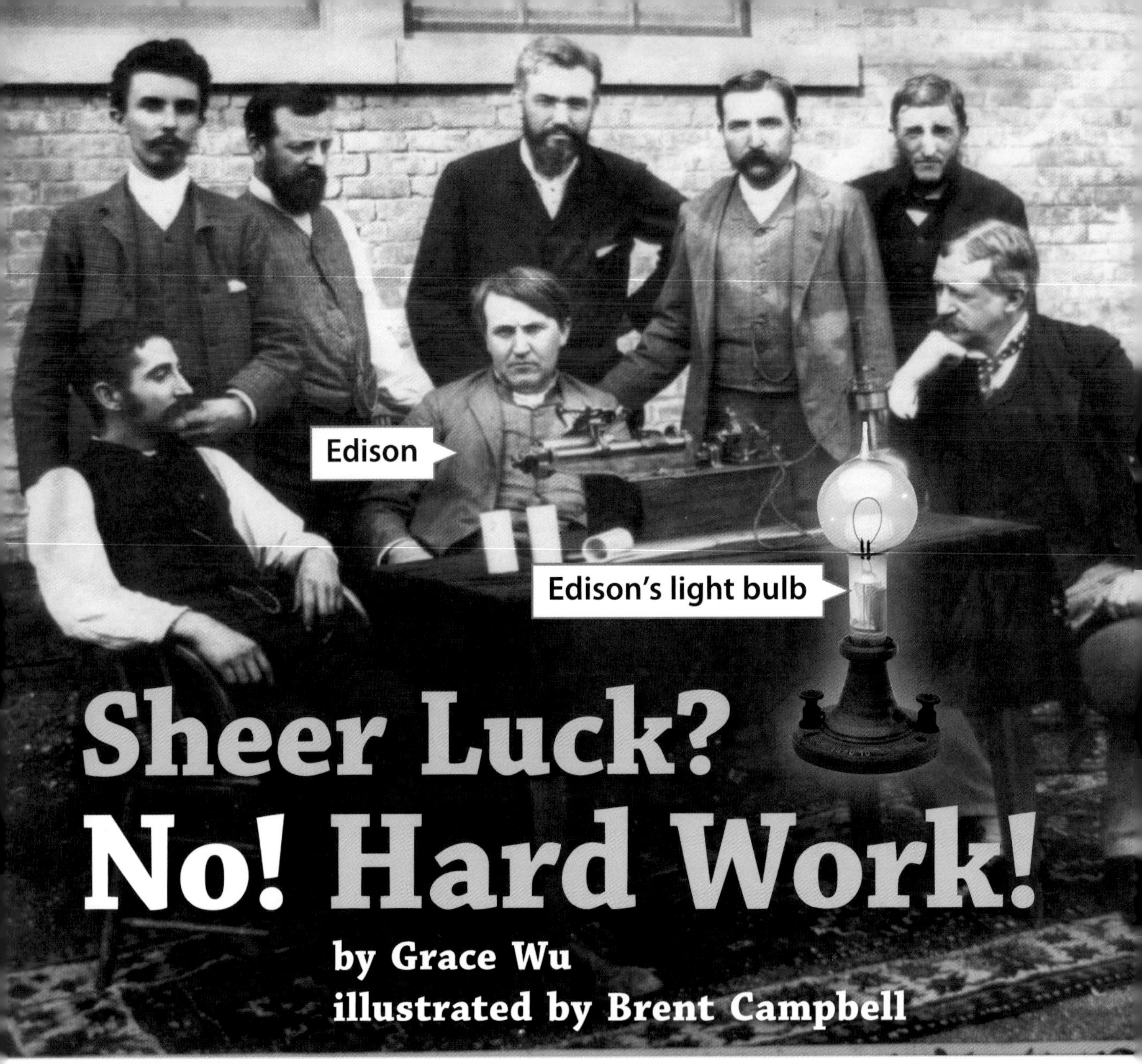

Sheer Luck? No! Hard Work!

by Grace Wu
illustrated by Brent Campbell

Over the years, smart people have invented things to make our lives better. Thomas Edison and his team invented long-lasting light bulbs, so people could see at night.

People are always trying to make inventions better. Someone invented the hearing aid to help people who can't hear well. Over the years, hearing aids got better and better.

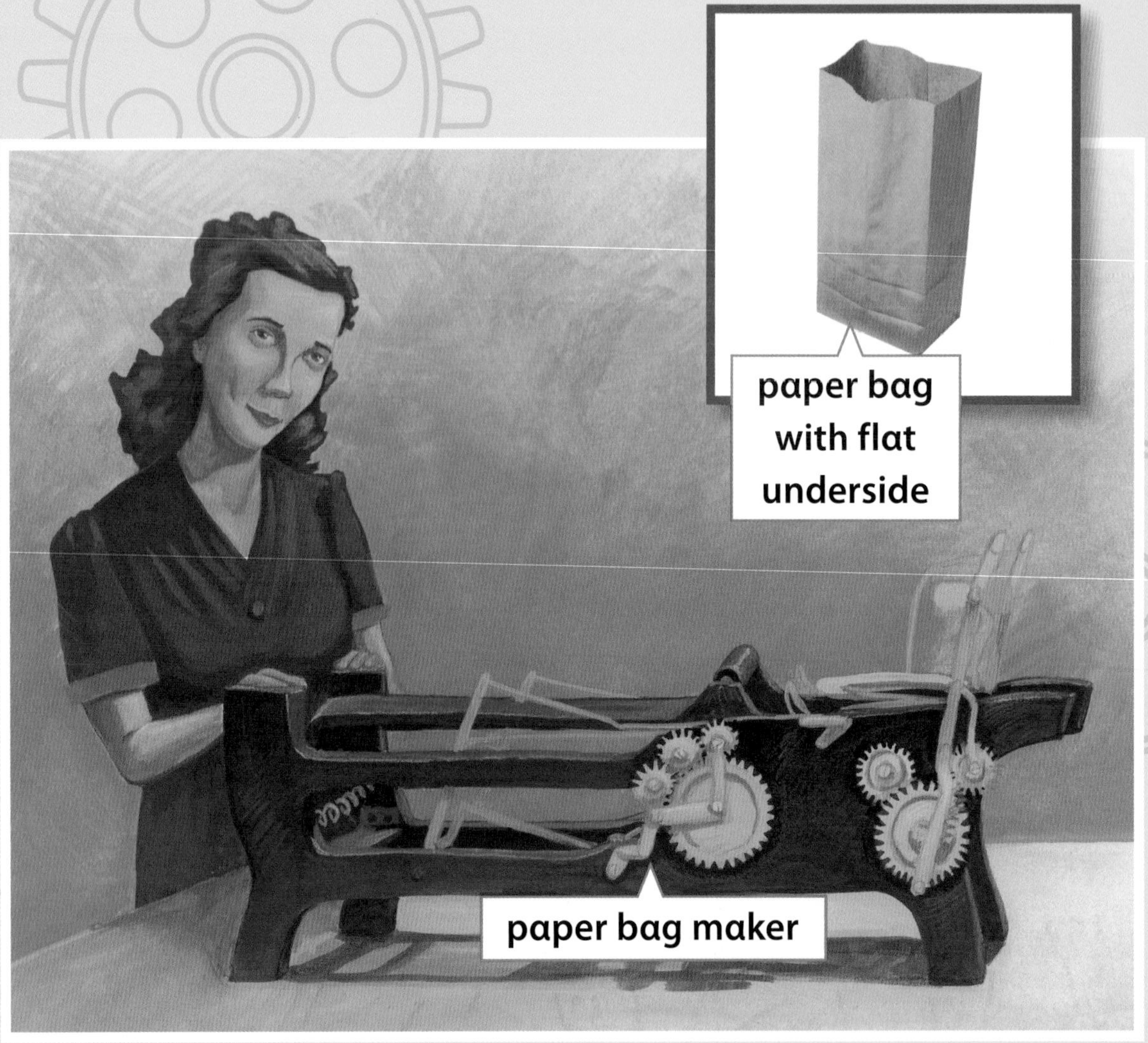

Margaret Knight invented a way to make paper bags with a flat underside that is still used.

You can invent things, too. Work on your own, in pairs, or in teams. You must work hard—day after weary day. It *may* take time to make something new. Maybe your first design fails. So does your second. Just keep trying.

Wilbur and Orville Wright

Wright brothers' first flight

1923 traffic light

It took nearly four years—and some crashes—for the Wright brothers to invent their airplane. Speaking of crashes, Garrett Morgan invented his traffic light in 1923 to prevent car crashes.

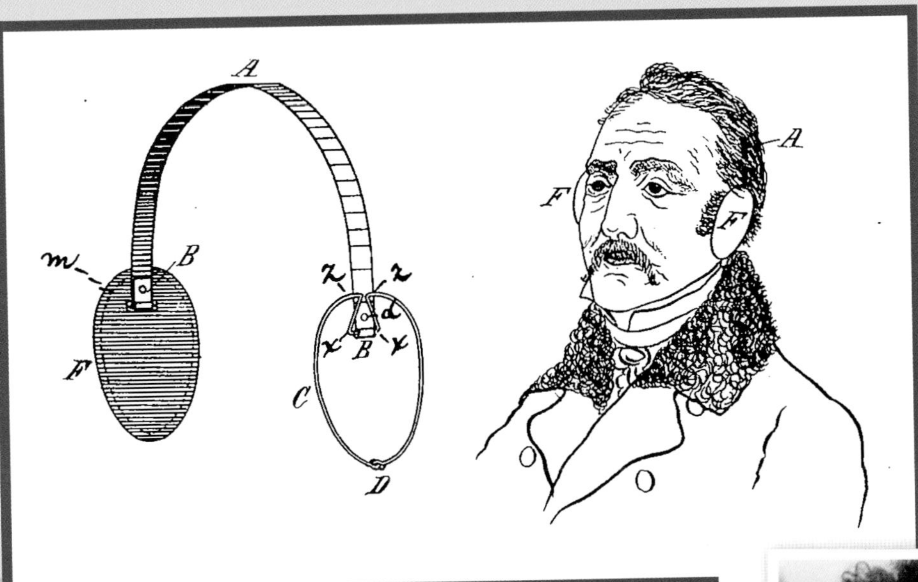

Chester Greenwood's earmuff invention

Do you have to be grown up to invent things? Chester Greenwood was 15 when he invented earmuffs to keep his ears warm.

Jean had been using a plastic step-stool to reach the sink. It was such a pain to use and store! Hearing about a school contest, Jean set to work. And she got the prize. Jean Low was five when she invented her kiddie stool!

A team of kids invented a way to change the flavor of foods. They thought kids steered away from good foods because of the flavors.

Would you like veggies that taste like spearmint or chocolate?

To invent something, start with a need. What's something people wish for? A steering wheel for bikes so they won't veer off the road? Clocks that play eerie music? Shears that cut rocks? Paint that won't smear?

Work in a team. That way, you've got more people thinking. Plus, you can cheer each other up when things go wrong. And they will!

Many schools have contests each year. They give kids a problem to work on. Any team can enter. Does your team have the stuff to invent something cool? ❖

Words with <u>eer</u>, <u>ear</u>

Read these words.

spear	sing	deer	doll
cheer	hear	truck	steer

Find the words with **eer** and **ear**.
Use letters to build them.

s p e a r

Talk Together

A spear can sing.

These are four things some make-believe kids invented. Choose words from the box above to tell your partner about each one.

A Crazy Painting

This painting is filled with such strange things! Look at it with a partner. Take turns reading clues and pointing out answers.

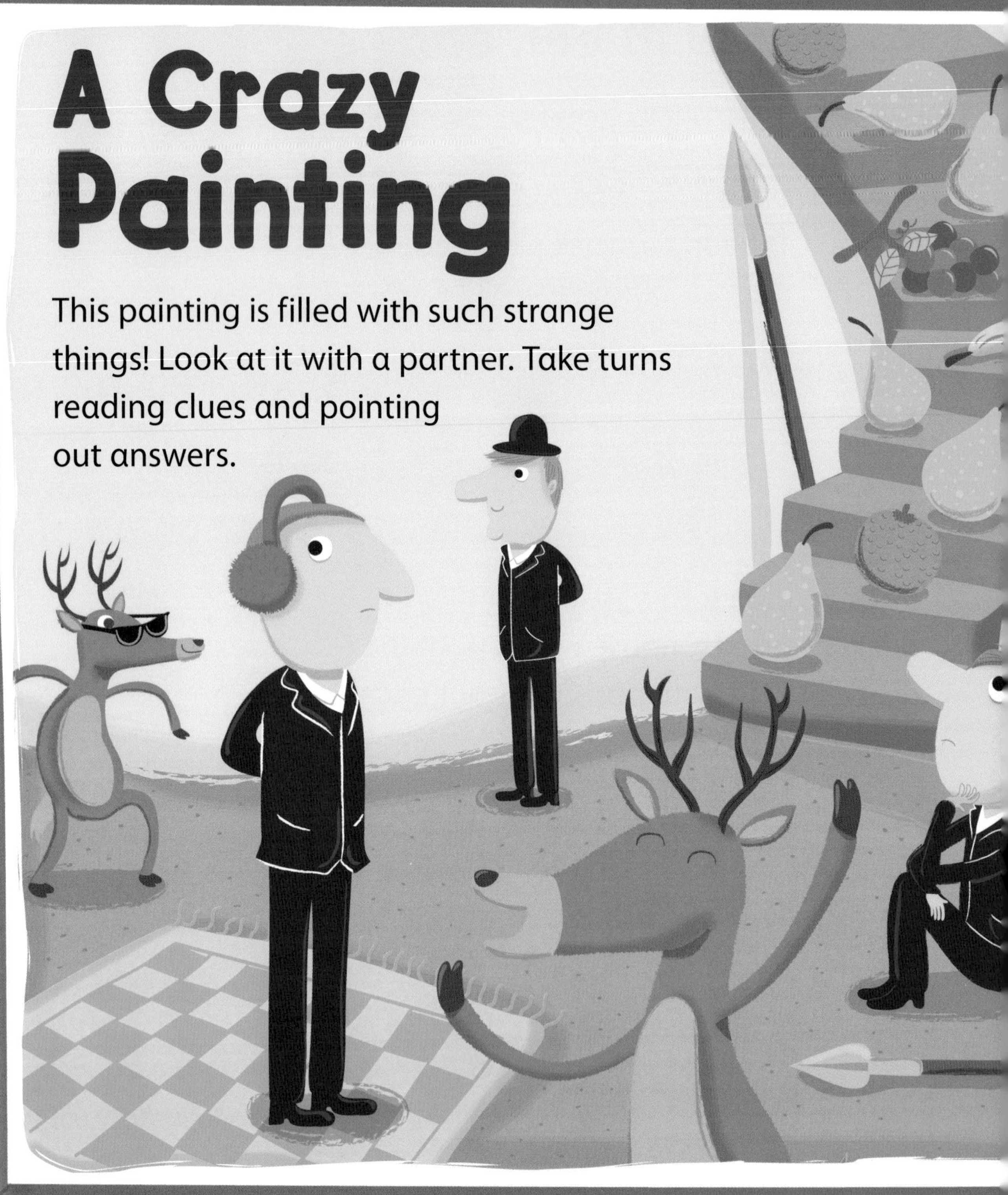

1. Find a teddy bear in an armchair.
2. Find a deer wearing a beard and earrings.
3. Find four men wearing earmuffs.
4. Find five pears on a staircase.
5. Find an animal that sees well at night.
6. Find a pair of squares near a spear.
7. Find a deer that cheers.

Acknowledgments
Grateful acknowledgment is given to the authors, artists, photographers, museums, publishers, and agents for permission to reprint copyrighted material. Every effort has been made to secure the appropriate permission. If any omissions have been made or if corrections are required, please contact the Publisher.

Photographic Credits
CVR Zave Smith/Corbis Super RF/Alamy Images. **2** (bl) Ragnc Kobanova/Shutterstock. (cl) Jupiterimages/age fotostock. (cr) Hintau Aliaksei/Shutterstock. (tl) cabania/Shutterstock. (tr) Denis Pepin/Shutterstock. **3** Liz Garza Williams/Hampton-Brown/National Geographic School Publishing. **4** (inset, t) The Granger Collection, New York. **5** David R. Frazier Photolibrary, Inc./Alamy Images. **6-7** Mapping Specialists. **8** Barrett Foster/Hampton-Brown/National Geographic School Publishing. **9** Barrett Foster/Hampton-Brown/National Geographic School Publishing. **10** Barrett Foster/Hampton-Brown/National Geographic School Publishing. **11** Barrett Foster/Hampton-Brown/National Geographic School Publishing. **12** Barrett Foster/Hampton-Brown/National Geographic School Publishing. **13** Barrett Foster/Hampton-Brown/National Geographic School Publishing. **14** (cr) Barrett Foster/Hampton-Brown/National Geographic School Publishing. (tl) Barrett Foster/Hampton-Brown/National Geographic School Publishing. **15** (bl) NZG/Shutterstock. (br) Rebecca Hale/Hampton-Brown/National Geographic School Publishing. (cr) Barrett Foster/Hampton-Brown/National Geographic School Publishing. (cr) Liz Garza Williams/Hampton-Brown/National Geographic School Publishing. **16** (bl) Digital Vision./Getty Images. (br) Ryan McVay/Getty Images. (cl) PhotoDisc/Getty Images. (cr) Péter Gudella/Shutterstock. (tl) Shane White/Shutterstock. (tr) Corel. **17** Liz Garza Williams/Hampton-Brown/National Geographic School Publishing. **18** (inset) SSPL/Getty Images. (t) Library of Congress Prints and Photographs Division Washington, D.C. 20540 USA, Reproduction No.: LC-USZ62-13413. **20** PeppPic/Shutterstock. **21** Andersen Ross/Blend Images/Getty Images. **22** (c) Schenectady Museum; Hall of Electrical History Foundation/Corbis. (tl) Library of Congress, Prints and Photographs Division, LC-USZ62-65478. (tr) The Granger Collection, New York. **23** (cr) Jim Jordan Photography/Photographer's Choice/Getty Images. (tl) United States Patent and Trademark Office. **28** Michael Newman/PhotoEdit. **29** Liz Garza Williams/Hampton-Brown/National Geographic School Publishing.

Illustrator Credits
3, **17**, **29**, **30-31** Mattia Cerato; **19**, **20**, **24**, **25**, **26**, **27** Brent Campbell

National Geographic School Publishing
Hampton-Brown
www.NGSP.com

Printed in the USA.
Quad Graphics, Leominster, MA

ISBN:978-0-7362-8079-2

17 18 19
10 9 8 7 6 5